W9-BSS-082

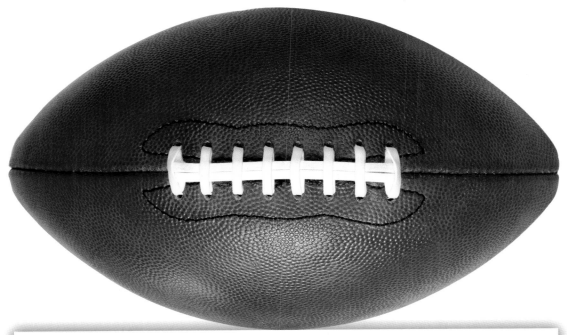

PEYTON MANNING
NFL MVP AND CHAMPION

The Child's World®

Published by The Child's World®
1980 Lookout Drive • Mankato, MN 56003-1705
800-599-READ • www.childsworld.com

ACKNOWLEDGMENTS
The Child's World®: Mary Berendes, Publishing Director
Red Line Editorial: Editorial direction
The Design Lab: Design
Amnet: Production
Design Elements: Todd Taulman/Shutterstock Images
Photographs ©: David Drapkin/AP Images, cover; Rich
Gabrielson/Icon SMI, 5; Yearbook Library, 7; Mark Humphrey/
AP Images, 9; Adam Nadel/AP Images, 11; Ron Schwane/
AP Images, 13; Anthony Correia/Shutterstock Images, 15;
Lynne Sladky/AP Images, 17; Mel Evans/AP Images, 19; Tony
Gutierrez/AP Images, 21

ISBN 9781631437380
LCCN 2014945443

Printed in the United States of America
Mankato, MN
November, 2014
PA02239

ABOUT THE AUTHOR

Maxwell Hammer grew up in the Adirondacks of New York before becoming an international sports reporter and children's book author. When not traveling the world on assignment, he spends his winters in Thunder Bay, Ontario, with his wife and pet beagle.

TABLE OF CONTENTS

CHAPTER 1

A TRUE LEADER

Peyton Manning takes his place behind the center. He waves his arms to point out what he sees from the defense. Then he barks orders.

The center snaps the ball. Manning puts his plans into action.

Denver Broncos fans never have to worry about Manning being prepared. He comes into each game ready. He knows what he needs to do. He knows what the other team plans to do. And then he leads the way for his team. It's no surprise that Manning's teams usually win.

Manning yells calls before plays. Some calls change the play. Others direct teammates. And some calls are just to trick the defense. Manning's most famous dummy call is the word "Omaha."

Manning calls the play during a 38-3 win over the
Kansas City Chiefs on December 30, 2012.

CHAPTER 2

ARCHIE'S SON

Peyton is from New Orleans, Louisiana. His dad, Archie Manning, was a star quarterback. He played for the National Football League's (NFL's) New Orleans Saints.

Peyton played with his brothers Eli and Cooper growing up. All three were great players in high school. Peyton was the starting quarterback for three years at Isidore Newman High School. Already he showed a strong passing arm. Some groups even named Peyton the national high school player of the year.

Peyton was also a great baseball and basketball player. He earned **varsity** letters in those sports in addition to football.

Manning showed his pro potential from a young age.

TENNESSEE BOUND

Many thought Peyton would play college football for Ole Miss. That's where Archie Manning played. But Peyton went his own way. He decided to play for the University of Tennessee Volunteers.

The Volunteers' starting quarterback was injured in the team's fourth game Peyton's freshman year. So Peyton stepped in. He was a natural leader. He led his team to seven wins in eight starts. Peyton and the Volunteers went 23-3 during Peyton's sophomore and junior years. The Volunteers came close to winning the national championship both years. NFL **scouts** were impressed by his play. Many people thought he would have been the top pick in that year's NFL **Draft**. But Peyton decided to stay at Tennessee for his senior season.

Peyton earned his college degree in speech communication after just three years. He graduated from Tennessee with honors.

Peyton set many passing records. But his senior year ended in disappointment. He just missed out on winning the Heisman Trophy, awarded each year to the best college player. And Tennessee again fell just short of a national title.

Manning runs for a touchdown to help the Volunteers to a 30-27 win over the Georgia Bulldogs on September 9, 1995.

FIRST TO LAST

Life moved quickly for Manning. His Volunteers lost in the Orange Bowl on January 2, 1998. The NFL Draft was less than four months later. The Indianapolis Colts selected him with the first overall pick.

Indianapolis had the first pick because the team struggled in 1997. Peyton stepped in as the starter right away as a **rookie**. He got a lot of valuable experience. But he did not win very many games. Indianapolis finished 3–13.

Manning set NFL rookie passing records for completions (326), attempts (575), yards (3,739), and touchdowns (26).

The Indianapolis Colts drafted Manning first overall in an effort to turn the team around after an awful season.

CHAPTER 5

BUILDING A JUGGERNAUT

Manning had a great attitude. He worked hard to understand the game. The Colts turned around in his second season.

Manning and wide receiver Marvin Harrison made a strong team. They led the Colts to the playoffs with a 13–3 record. The Colts made the playoffs in six of Manning's first eight seasons.

Those teams became known for their great offenses. Manning passed for an NFL-record 49 touchdowns in 2004. He won his second consecutive Most Valuable Player (MVP) Award. But the Colts struggled to win big games in the playoffs.

Manning met Ashley Thompson the summer before his freshman year at Tennessee. They were married in 2001 and had twins in 2011.

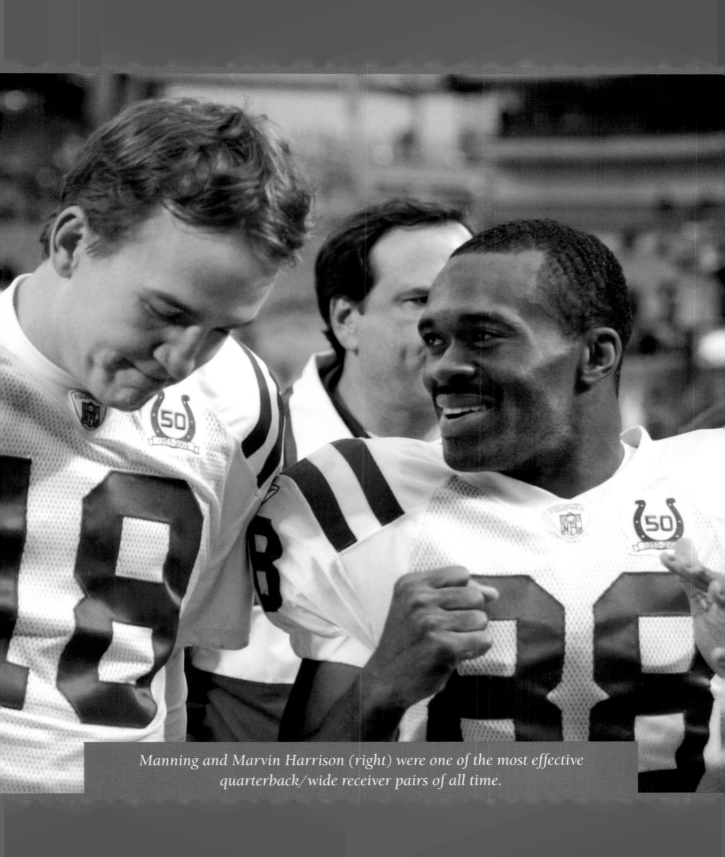

Manning and Marvin Harrison (right) were one of the most effective quarterback/wide receiver pairs of all time.

CHAPTER 6

CHAMPION AT LAST

The 2006 Colts got off to a fast start. They won their first nine games. The offense was among the league's best. And Manning was again great. He led the league with 31 touchdown passes. He had the NFL's best **quarterback rating** for the third year in a row.

The Colts faced the New England Patriots in the conference championship. The Patriots had ended the Colts' season in the 2003 and 2004 playoffs. Now they took an 18-point lead.

This time, Manning led a comeback. A late, 80-yard touchdown drive put the Colts up for good. They won 38–34. Two weeks later, they faced the Chicago Bears in the Super Bowl. Manning picked apart the Bears' defense with expert passes. The Colts won 29–17. Manning was not just a champion. He was also the Super Bowl MVP.

n's brother Eli Manning
on to play quarterback
e New York Giants. He
em to two Super Bowl
hrough 2013.

Manning (18) talks to his Colts teammates during their 29-17 Super Bowl win over the Chicago Bears on February 4, 2007.

CHAPTER 7

STAYING ON TOP

Winning a championship made Manning a legend. But he continued to work as hard as ever. Manning watched hours of game video. That helped him understand both his offense and opposing defenses. His skills and knowledge showed on the field. He won two more MVP awards in 2008 and 2009. He led the Colts back to the playoffs every year from 2007 to 2010. Indianapolis even reached the Super Bowl after the 2009 season. However, they lost to the New Orleans Saints.

Manning didn't miss a start from 1998–2010. However, he suffered a neck injury. Offseason surgery did not go as planned. More surgery followed. Manning ended up missing the entire 2011 season.

Manning started 208 consecutive regular-season games from 1998 through 2010. Only Brett Favre started more games at quarterback. Favre started 297 games from 1992 to 2010.

Manning hands off the ball to Joseph Addai during the Colts' 31-17 loss to the New Orleans Saints in the February 7, 2010 Super Bowl.

THE LONG ROAD BACK

Few people knew it, but Manning was struggling in 2011. He could barely hold the football. When he tried to throw, his passes were weak. The great quarterback had to accept that his career might be over.

The Colts won just two games without Manning in 2011. Manning worked tirelessly to be ready for the 2012 season. But the Colts decided to release Manning and draft a new quarterback.

Quarterbacks like Manning aren't often **free agents**. Teams lined up to sign him. He decided to head west and play for the Denver Broncos.

Manning's arm was so weak in the fall of 2011 that he couldn't throw a dart hard enough to stick into a dartboard.

Peyton Manning and younger brother Eli (left) have played three games against each other in the NFL. Peyton's teams have won all three "Manning Bowls."

CHAPTER 9

BUCKING BRONCO

Broncos fans welcomed Manning. He gave those fans plenty to cheer about. His passes didn't quite have the zip they did before. But Manning knew just when and where to throw the ball. His 37 touchdown passes in 2012 were the second most in his career. But the Broncos lost in the playoffs.

Manning came back better than ever in 2013. His 55 passing touchdowns were an NFL record. So were his 5,477 passing yards. No one was surprised when Manning won his fifth MVP award. Behind Manning, the Broncos had the league's best offense. They won 13 games and reached the Super Bowl.

Manning makes an effort to give back to the community. He works with young football players at the Manning Passing Academy. Manning also established the PeyBack Foundation to support disadvantaged youth in Colorado, Indiana, Louisiana, and Tennessee.

The season ended with a disappointing 43-8 loss in the Super Bowl to the Seattle Seahawks. For a quarterback who could barely throw two years earlier, it was a season for the ages. But for Manning, it was just motivation to keep getting better.

Manning gets ready to pass against the Dallas Cowboys on October 6, 2013.

FUN FACTS

PEYTON MANNING

BORN: March 24, 1976

HOMETOWN: New Orleans, Louisiana

TEAMS: Indianapolis Colts (1998–2011), Denver Broncos (2012–)

POSITION: Quarterback

HEIGHT: 6′5″

WEIGHT: 230 pounds

NFL DEBUT: September 6, 1998

SUPER BOWLS (WINS IN BOLD): XLI, February 4, 2007;
   XLIV, February 7, 2010; XLVIII, February 2, 2014

AWARDS
   NFL MVP: 2003, 2004, 2008, 2009, 2013

GLOSSARY

draft (draft) Professional teams scout and select new players to join their rosters in the draft. Peyton Manning was selected first overall in the 1998 NFL Draft.

free agents (free AY-juhnts) Players who are not signed to a team are free agents. Manning got a lot of attention when he became a free agent in 2012.

quarterback rating (KWOR-tur-bak RAY-ting) The quarterback rating is a formula to determine a quarterback's play based on completions, yards, touchdowns, and interceptions per attempt. Manning had the highest quarterback rating in the NFL from 2004–2006.

rookie (RUK-ee) A player in his or her first year in a new league is a rookie. Peyton Manning was a star rookie quarterback for the Colts.

scouts (skouts) People who watch football games and evaluate talent are scouts. Scouts were impressed by Manning's play with the Tennessee Volunteers.

varsity (VAHR-si-tee) The varsity team is the top team in each sport at a high school. Manning played varsity basketball, baseball, and football.

TO LEARN MORE

BOOKS

DiPrimio, Peter. *Peyton Manning*. Kennett Square, PA: Purple Toad Pub., 2015.

Nagle, Jeanne. *Archie, Peyton, and Eli Manning: Football's Royal Family*. New York: Rosen Central, 2010.

Wyner, Zach. *Denver Broncos*. New York: AV2 by Weigl, 2014.

WEB SITES

Visit our Web site for links about Peyton Manning:
childsworld.com/links

Note to Parents, Teachers, and Librarians: We routinely verify our Web links to make sure they are safe and active sites. So encourage your readers to check them out!

INDEX